Herda, D.J.
AUTHOR
ENViRONMENTAL AMERICA
TITLE
The NORTH Central States

Environmental
AMERICA

Environmental
AMERICA

The North Central States

by
D.J. Herda

The Millbrook Press
Brookfield, CT
The American Scene

Cover photographs (clockwise from top) courtesy of
Wisconsin Division of Tourism Development

Inside photographs courtesy of
Wisconsin Division of Tourism Development: 6, 10, 16, 20, 36, 48; D. J. Herda: 13, 24,
33; Wisconsin Dept. of Natural Resources: 14, 27, 28, 30, 41, 44, 54; Environmental
Protection Agency: 19, 50

Designed by Moonlit Ink, Madison, WI 53705
Illustrations by Renee Graef

Cataloging-in-Publication Data
Herda, D. J.
Environmental America: The North Central States.
Brookfield, CT, The Millbrook Press. 1991.
64 p.;   col. ill.; (The American Scene)
Includes bibliographical references and index.
Summary: The impact of humankind and society on the environment, with special
emphasis on the North Central region.
ISBN 1-878841-08-4   639.9 HER

1. North Central states--environmental impacts--juvenile literature. 2. Conservation
of natural resources. 3. Pollution. [1. Environmental America: The North Central
States] I Title. II. Series.

C O N T E N T S

Introduction
7

The Web of Life
11

The Land We Walk
17

The Air We Breathe
31

The Water We Drink
37

A Time For Action
45

What We Can Do
51

For More Information
55

Notes
58

Glossary
59

Bibliography
62

Index
63

INTRODUCTION

The land of the North Central United States is as diverse as any on Earth. As you pass through the states of North and South Dakota, you see mile after mile of open rangeland. In Nebraska, Iowa, Wisconsin, and Illinois, cornstalks as high as a man's shoulders wave endlessly in the wind. In Minnesota and Michigan's Upper Peninsula, ponds, rivers, streams, and lakes by the thousands glisten beneath a crystal clear sky. In Indiana, Ohio, and Michigan's Lower Peninsula, great fields of waving wheat bump shoulders with fruit orchards and vineyards.

The temperatures throughout the North Central region range from scorching hot in summer to frigid cold in winter—among the coldest anywhere in the continental United States. But the region is breathtakingly beautiful with its endless expanse of flatlands, gently rolling hills, and steep river valleys.

Water is everywhere here—the sprawling Great Lakes, which make up the largest freshwater reserve in the world; the mighty Mississippi River, which dissects the country from north to south; the St. Lawrence Seaway, which empties the Great Lakes into the northern Atlantic Ocean; and millions of farm ponds, glacial kettle holes, country streams, and backwater wetlands.

When nighttime comes, the Earth opens to a litany of wonderful sounds. Bat wings flutter in the thick summer air. Owls summon their distant mates. Tree frogs and ground toads split the solitude of darkness with their calls. Kit foxes and coyotes howl at the moon.

(opposite page)
Glistening blue water is just one of the attractions of the North Central region.

IN THE BEGINNING

The upper Midwest, as it's sometimes called, is composed of several different environments, or biomes. The northernmost range of North Dakota, Minnesota, Wisconsin, and Michigan boasts mile after mile of pine tree forests. Indiana, Illinois, Ohio, Iowa, southern Wisconsin, and southern Minnesota include large stands of hardwoods such as oaks, maples, and elms. And all the North Central states have at least some grasslands.

This is a much different environment than existed when the Earth was formed more than 4.5 billion years ago. Back then, there were no trees, no lakes, no seaways. There were no birds or mammals, grass or flowers. There was nothing, in fact, except scorching hot rock, a few basic gases, and a little water vapor. But in time, they combined to produce a simple atmosphere from which the very first life on Earth emerged.

As Earth's earliest aquatic plants were born and began to grow, they gave off oxygen. The oxygen that the plants produced was held close to the Earth's surface by the planet's gravitational pull. As oxygen and other gases were exposed to the forces of wind, water, and sunlight, a more complex atmosphere capable of sustaining higher life forms evolved.

Although the actual beginnings of life on Earth are unclear, fossil records show a rich heritage of slowly evolving life forms: giant mosses and ferns, ancient cattails and grasses, slugs and worms, fishes and reptiles.

Over the millions of years in which life on Earth has existed, its biosphere, those places collectively capable of supporting life, has undergone numerous changes. Seas have formed and dried up. Mountains have risen and eroded away. Entire continents have shifted position, opening and closing pathways for Earth's migrating wildlife.

Great ice glaciers have come and gone, carving in their wake the upper Midwest's five Great Lakes and countless potholes and kettles, or small, deep depressions that filled with water as the ice receded. By the time the last of the great ice ages covered much of North America, the dinosaurs that once walked the Earth had all but become extinct, replaced by other animal species better suited to withstand a changing environment.

But where in this evolutionary portrait of life was humankind?

If you were to watch a 30-minute television program about the chronological history of life on Earth, you'd see the minute-by-minute development of breathtakingly beautiful mosses, lichens, ferns, and grasses. These would be followed by strange and remarkable animals in the seas, animals that eventually grew legs and began breathing air into amazingly complex organs called lungs.

As the show continued, you'd witness the evolution of reptiles and the development of dinosaurs followed by both small and large mammals. You'd see animals flying through the air and crawling on the ground, climbing over rocks and swinging through trees.

Finally, in the last 3.5 seconds of the program, you'd witness the birth and entire history of humankind!

It may be difficult to believe that modern Homo sapiens, or human beings, have populated the planet for so short a period of time—approximately 40,000 of its billions of years of existence—but it's true.[1] Yet human beings have made more of an impact on the planet than any other creature since the beginning of life itself.

Some of that impact has been positive, but much more of it has been negative. In the relatively short blink of a geological eye, humankind has managed to change the Earth's biosphere so that it no longer functions smoothly. In the process, the atmosphere has been fouled with chemicals; the water, with organic, agricultural, and industrial wastes; and the land, with heavy metals and toxic poisons.

For the first time in history, nearly all the plant and animal species that inhabit the Earth—including humans—are in danger.

THE WEB OF LIFE

Life in America's North Central region exists in every conceivable nook and cranny. Giant oak trees and spiraling jack pines tower above the landscape. Sightless fish live, breed, and die in frigid pools deep inside caves untouched by sunlight. Gophers, badgers, groundhogs, and other burrowing mammals cut tunnels through the prairie lands. Ferns, mosses, and lichens grow in the shade of great forests and modest woods.

Although various plant and animal species have come and gone over the millions of years of Earth's existence, their rate of decline has accelerated most within the last half century. Plants and animals in America's North Central states have been particularly vulnerable.

THE NORTH CENTRAL BIOMES

Earth's plants and animals have gradually evolved as part of a living system, called a biome, in which all of life is interrelated. The largest biomes consist of grasslands, tropical rain forests, deciduous forests, coniferous forests, tundras, and deserts. Each biome varies greatly in climate and physical makeup.

The North Central region of the United States, with its native grasslands, rolling hills, running waterways, and deciduous and coniferous forests, once held the promise of new wealth to families willing to cross the mighty Allegheny Mountains of the East and head west toward the plains. But early pioneers moving out of the eastern forest belt were disappointed by the tallgrass prairies they discovered in Ohio and Illinois. They were afraid that the region's treelessness,

(opposite page)
Great hardwood forests once covered much of the region's land.

which they took to mean a lack of soil fertility, meant poor farming. They were afraid even more that the Indian-haunted plains beyond Wisconsin and Iowa, which they called "the Great American Desert," were barren and lifeless.

But their fears were short-lived. With 8-foot bluestem, Indian, switch, and slough grasses, the tallgrass prairies soon proved to be the finest croplands in the world, ideally suited to the corn and wheat—both grasses themselves—that the settlers hoped to grow.

The lands of the North Central region were made to order for farming—worked over first by ancient glaciers that left in their wake vast mineral deposits, then mulched and fertilized by one generation after another of wild animals and plants. The grounds were regularly "plowed" by gophers, ground squirrels, and badgers and fertilized by bison, elk, and deer until rich black topsoil lay 2 feet thick beneath the grass.

CULTIVATING THE PRAIRIE LANDS

But cultivating the prairie lands was easier said than done. The sod was tough, and traditional plows broke or stuck in the masses of tangled roots and sticky humus. By the 1830s, though, new plows made of specially polished steel were slicing through the roots and folding the tough sod back for planting, and America's breadbasket was born.[1]

By the mid-1800s, new, more efficient means of transportation—railroads, riverboats, and refrigerator cars—had opened new markets for North Central wheat, corn, and beef. Cattle grazed contentedly on the high-protein grasslands and the stubble from cornstalks following the harvest. All the while, North Central farmers rich with prosperity turned ever larger fields of sod into more productive croplands. And an increasing supply of high-quality grains and beef poured back into the cities of the East.

(opposite page)
While the beef cattle industry is important to the region's economy, it has also been destructive to the environment.

As the prairie lands of the upper Midwest continued falling to the plow, hardy pioneers slowly worked their way westward onto the great plains of Nebraska and into North and South Dakota. Spurred on by the Homestead Act of 1862, which granted 160 acres of federal land to anyone who farmed the plains for at least five years, the pioneers hoped to estab-

Once groundcover is destroyed, various forms of erosion take their toll on topsoil.

lish successful farming communities similar to the ones they left behind in Ohio, Illinois, and Wisconsin.

SMALL HOMESTEADS FAIL

But a 160-acre plot soon proved to be insufficient in a land where unirrigated soils were as likely to dry up and blow away in the wind as they were to produce grain, and many homesteads failed. The Homestead Act was later amended to grant larger parcels of land to plains farmers who purchased tractors and other mechanized farm implements to increase farm production. But the tractors merely compacted the already dry soil, making it even more vulnerable to erosion.

Ranchers, too, were soon drawn to the plains, as much by their stark beauty and endless horizons as by the quality of their grasslands. But they also met with problems. Summer droughts and winter blizzards killed much of their livestock. In an attempt to recover their losses, they began grazing more stock than the grass could support. Before long, overgrazing took its toll.

The winds that whipped across the open plains picked up valuable topsoil, no longer anchored by the roots of native grasses, and scattered it across the countryside. Sudden rains resulted in flash floods that washed much of the remaining topsoil away. Rivers and streams that once ran clear and clean soon clogged with silt. Weeds such as star thistles and poisonous Klamath spread over huge areas.

Throughout it all, homesteaders by the tens of thousands, each eager to claim a share of free land, continued pouring onto the plains. In 1914, as war raged in Europe, the demand for food increased. More homesteaders moved west, more plows broke ground, and more native grasslands gave out under the pressure.

THE DUST BOWL IS BORN

Then, in the 1930s, the droughts came—month after month of little or no rain. Sprawling fields of wheat, oats, rye, and corn withered and died. Increasing soil erosion produced huge windswept clouds of dust. Within a matter of months, some of the richest, most fertile topsoil the world had ever seen had vanished in the wind, and the Dust Bowl—the worst agricultural disaster in the history of America—was born.

Tens of thousands of North Central farmers and ranchers—unable to meet their mortgages—lost their farms, ranches, and homes and were forced to move. Many took newspaperman Horace Greeley's advice to "Go west, young man, go west" and settled as far west as California. Alone and impoverished, they joined crews of migrant farm workers or became miners, loggers, or fishermen.[2] And as the soil disappeared from the upper Midwest, so, too, did the habitats for thousands of insects, birds, reptiles, amphibians, and mammals that had once made the grasslands their home.

CHAPTER TWO

THE LAND
WE WALK

Even with the widespread destruction of the environment in the North Central states, wildlife throughout the upper Midwest is abundant, from white-tailed deer and black bear to red and gray fox, coyotes, great barred owls, red-tailed hawks, bluejays, mourning doves, and finches. But the number of species is dwindling, and one of the main reasons is the economic backbone of the Midwest—agriculture.

MONOCULTURE AND FARMING

During the early to mid-1800s, farmers throughout the North Central region of the country upset the delicate balance of nature by moving onto the land, clearing forests, and plowing up hundreds of thousands of acres. To make matters worse, they began using a farming practice called monoculture.

Monoculture, the cultivation of large stretches of land with a single crop such as corn or wheat, became popular in the upper Midwest before the turn of the century because of mechanized farming. By planting only one crop, a farmer had only to worry about one planting time, one fertilizing time, and one harvesting time. It proved to be an efficient way to make use of expensive farm machinery while reducing labor costs. Polyculture, or the cultivation of a field with more than one crop, requires greater expenditures of time and machinery.

(opposite page)
Most North Central region farmers today practice monoculture, which can destroy valuable soil nutrients.

But as farmers throughout the upper Midwest moved steadily toward one-crop farming, they discovered an alarming pattern. Their monocrops were slowly robbing the land of crucial nutrients, forcing farmers to increase the application of manure and chemical fertilizers, often at great expense.

They discovered, too, that insect infestations were becoming more frequent and severe. As a result, they were forced to turn to increased applications of expensive insecticides to protect their crops.

Then they found that weeds tended to proliferate in one-crop fields, so they began using shallow tilling and other methods to control the weeds. But these methods stole nutrients and precious moisture from crops.

As the practice of monoculture spread throughout the North Central states, farm profits fell due to increased fertilizer and pesticide costs. To compensate for rising costs, farmers began planting more and more land, often on such marginally productive terrain as hillsides, recently cleared woodlands, and wetlands.

OUR DIMINISHING HABITAT

The results of such agricultural abuse throughout the upper Midwest are frightening. Much of what once had been the richest, loamiest soil in the world has disappeared into thin air, blown away on hot summer winds and washed away by rain and spring thaws. Many prairie soils that once held up to 250 tons of rich humus per acre (as opposed to 20 to 50 tons in forestlands) have been reduced to worthless scrublands barely able to sustain any growth at all.

Many varieties of beneficial insects and burrowing animals have already disappeared from beneath the soil. With them have gone such carnivorous predators as badgers, foxes, hawks, owls, eagles, coyotes, and timber wolves. Yet the abuse continues.

(opposite page)
Crop dusting for insect control is an ineffective and unsound practice that has environmentalists concerned.

Several days each summer in Grafton, North Dakota, the streetlights come on at noon, and motorists are forced to drive with their headlights on. Some stop their cars because they can't see the road. The cause? Dust storms—the worst many locals have ever seen, even during the peak of the Dust Bowl days of the 1930s.

Only three times since the Dust Bowl days have North Central farms and ranches lost more topsoil to drought and winds than in the spring of 1988. North Dakota's fertile Red River valley lost an average of 15 tons of topsoil an acre, with

18

some losses exceeding 30 tons. Anything over 5 tons an acre is considered excessive.

LOWER CROP YIELDS

As the 1988 crop year ended, farmers were disappointed with the low yields from their drought-stricken fields. "We have 14 million acres of bare ground," said Carl Fanning, a researcher at North Dakota State University. "Every time the wind blows more than 12 miles an hour, there's going to be dust—still more of our topsoil—in the air."

One North Dakota conservationist agreed. "Landowners aren't only concerned about losing their crops. They're also concerned about losing their soil, because that's the real source of their livelihood."

What's worse, water erosion by winter rains and spring runoff not only robs the land of its topsoil, it also increases the high levels of sediment in rivers, lakes, and streams.

The U.S. Department of Agriculture estimates today that nearly one third of all North Central cropland is seriously affected by some form of erosion, and much of the land may soon have to be taken out of production. As a result, crop yields in the upper Midwest are expected to drop by 25 to 30 percent by the year 2030. In Illinois, average grain yields fell 2 percent in the five-year period between 1979 and 1984 and are expected to continue falling as some of the state's most productive farmland disappears upwind and downriver.

CONGRESSIONAL ACTION

During the late 1970s and early 1980s, high farm prices and booming exports spurred farmers in the Midwest to expand and, in the process, take on more and more debt. As speculators purchased vast expanses of land for planting wheat and corn, millions of acres of ill-suited land were placed into crop production. The resulting soil erosion soon rivaled that of the Dust Bowl years, despite federal spending of nearly $2 billion a year for erosion control.

In 1985, Congress passed a bill that gave soil conservation top priority. The bill withheld federal funds from farmers who

(opposite page)
Contour plowing is one of many ways to prevent soil erosion.

21

failed to take proper care of their lands. The law included a special "swampbuster" provision to remove environmentally sensitive wetlands from crop production. The law also established a federally backed conservation fund. The fund makes payments each year to farmers who plant their most erodible fields with grasses and trees, keeping them out of crop production for a minimum of ten years.

So far, the results are promising. Nearly 9 million acres of erodible land entered the reserve in 1986 alone, most of it in the North Central United States. But nearly 1 million farmers will need to develop and implement approved conservation plans by 1995 in order to qualify for federal benefits and make the plan work. Not all farmers favor the plan. Many feel it's a not-so-subtle form of governmental blackmail aimed at controlling U.S. agriculture.

THE COST OF AGRICULTURAL CHEMICALS

Soil erosion isn't the only environmental problem facing the upper Midwest. Millions of tons of agricultural chemicals each year run off croplands and into the area's lakes and streams. These chemicals stimulate the growth of algae, gradually destroying the oxygen on which aquatic life thrives.

Cattle destined for market grow fat in huge feedlots in Illinois, Iowa, Nebraska, and South Dakota while creating enormous waste-disposal problems. Pesticides applied to fields sometimes kill off beneficial plants, animals, and insects in the process. Irrigation results in high concentrations of salt in the topsoil—salt that's toxic to both plants and animals.

STRIPPING THE LAND

The energy industry, too, is a polluter of North Central land, especially in the coal-rich areas of Ohio, Indiana, and southern Illinois. Extracting coal to meet our nation's rising energy demands is both costly and damaging to the environment.

Coal in the upper Midwest is most often extracted by a method known as strip-mining. Strip-mining uses giant earth-gouging machines to remove the surface layers of soil and rock and uncover large seams of coal.

World Land Area Suitable for Agriculture

No Limitations	11%
Too Wet	10%
Too Shallow	22%
Chemical Problems	23%
Too Dry	28%
Unaccounted	6%

Satellite topographical studies show that, of all the world's land, very little is actually suitable for agricultural use.

Source: Essam, El-Hinnawi and Mansur, Hashmi, *The State of the Environment* (London: Butterworths, 1987), p. 36

Each year throughout the United States, an area twice the size of the District of Columbia is strip-mined. These mines result in "a chemical and physical decomposition of the soil which restricts land utilization for agriculture and may affect the land's capability to support any vegetation whatsoever," according to a report by the Government Accounting Office (GAO). But coal producers know that strip-mining is three times more profitable than underground mining, so they continue to push for more strip mines.

Recently passed federal laws require strip-mining companies to repair the damage they do to the land. But those repairs, say environmentalists, are superficial at best. They're designed to make the ground look better, but they fail to address the most serious problems that strip-mining causes, such as the leaching of toxic chemicals and other solutions into nearby soils, surface waterways, and groundwater systems.

ENCROACHING CIVILIZATION

Urban sprawl is another problem facing the upper Midwest. As people move out of towns and cities and into the country, they often end up destroying some of the nation's most environmentally sensitive or agriculturally productive lands in the process.

Southern Illinois' Cache Basin Swamp once covered more than a quarter of a million acres of the state near the lower Ohio River. When naturalist John James Audubon visited it in 1810, he found passenger pigeons, ivory-billed woodpeckers, wolves, cougars, and black bears—all gone now from the state's wilderness.

Gone, too, is most of the swamp itself—drained, ditched, logged, diverted, and filled in with sediment by advancing civilization until only a "wetland on the brink" remains, according to environmental activist and Southern Illinois University zoologist Ann Phillippi. "There is potential for recovery," she says, "but an equal chance we may lose the swamp completely."

The loss of the swamp would be a loss for all of us, since it contains record specimens of green hawthorn, water locust, water tupelo trees, and bald cypress—some more than a thousand years old. The swamp is also home to such endangered or threatened animals as the eastern ribbon snake and the cypress darter, both of which until recently had been presumed extinct in Illinois.

In order to reduce the damage to the swamp, the Nature Conservancy and the state are trying to acquire the remaining 10,000 acres of land. Unless they succeed, urban sprawl is likely to claim one more victim.

PROPOSED ST. LOUIS PROJECT

The region's valuable wetlands are continuing to disappear at an alarming rate.

In the nearby city of St. Louis, Missouri, built along the convergence of the Mississippi, Illinois, and Missouri rivers, local officials recently announced their intentions to build a commercial-industrial complex on more than 500 acres. Called Riverport, the project was to include a new 70,000-seat domed stadium for St. Louis' professional baseball team, the Cardinals.

But Riverport would have required the drying up of existing wetlands critical to natural habitat while destroying some of the area's best agricultural land, according to the East Missouri Sierra Club. Together with the Environmental Protection Agency (EPA) and the U.S. Fish and Wildlife Service, the club petitioned the Army Corps of Engineers for an environmental impact statement on the project.

The corps rejected the petition and in May 1985 issued developers a permit to build a levee and fill in wetlands at the development site. The following year, environmentalists and local citizens filed suit against the developers and the corps in order to halt development. In the meantime, the Sierra Club's Midwest Regional Conservation Committee asked for suggestions and support for the establishment of a Great Confluence Reserve to protect parts of the three rivers and their floodplains from unsound development. Until such a reserve is established, according to the Sierra Club, environmentalists will need to fight in the courts "every Missouri Bottom boondoggle that comes along."

THROWAWAY SOCIETY

America today is being buried beneath tons of garbage. In the 1920s, each U.S. citizen threw away an average of 2.75 pounds of waste a day. By 1985, that figure had risen to 4 pounds a day, excluding agricultural, mining, and industrial wastes.[1]

One of the most promising means of reducing the amount of waste to be disposed of is called recycling—removing those items that may have market value as new and useful materials. Discarded rubber tires, for instance, may be turned into pavement for new roads. Discarded newspapers may be turned into books, pamphlets, and writing tablets.

Although recycling isn't easy, it is effective, especially when recyclable materials are separated from nonrecyclable materials at their source: the homes, businesses, schools, and factories that generate the trash. But so far, few mandatory recycling laws exist, and voluntary recycling programs simply aren't enough. If the upper Midwest is going to come to grips with the problem, it will need governmental action similar to that which took place recently in the state of Wisconsin.

TOUGH NEW LAWS

Wisconsin's new recycling law will ban all recyclable waste from state landfills and incinerators by 1995; establish an $18.5 million fund to help the state's communities initiate recycling programs; create new programs for recycling education, market development, and law enforcement; and restrict waste brought into Wisconsin from other states.

The law is expected to reduce the amount of waste entering Wisconsin's landfills by 40 percent, which is far ahead of the EPA's goal of 25 percent. It's the toughest recycling law in the United States, banning more than a dozen items from disposal. This includes most paper products, yard waste, metal and plastic containers, and tires.

The provision in the law banning waste from other states is aimed at reducing the flow of wastes across state lines and inspiring neighboring states to pass stricter recycling laws of their own. Four Wisconsin state landfills currently receive nearly 450,000 tons of waste a year from five northern Illinois counties—an amount equal to 15 percent of Illinois' entire waste generation. With similar laws on their books, many North Central communities could lower their use of raw materials, reduce the need for additional incinerators and landfills, and create new jobs.

But recycling can't eliminate all the region's wastes. Some have to be disposed of in other manners. Toxic wastes from refineries, chemical plants, and industry are all too often discarded in manners that are destructive to the environment and dangerous to humankind.

THE TOXIC-WASTE PROBLEM

The EPA estimated in 1983 that there were 2,900 abandoned hazardous-waste sites in Region V, which includes Illinois, Indiana, Michigan, Minnesota, Ohio, and Wisconsin. By 1988, that number had grown to more than 5,300.

More than 36,000 companies in the region currently handle hazardous wastes, and nearly 1,000 facilities treat, store, or dispose of these wastes. Various federal laws passed in 1976 and 1984 were intended to minimize the threat of toxic wastes to

Toxic Substances Discharged by U.S. Industry, 1987

Destination	Millions of Pounds
Air	2700
Lakes, Rivers and Streams	550
Landfills and Earthen Pits	3900
Treatment and Disposal Facilities	3300
Total	10450

Source: Environmental Protection Agency, reported in *The Washington Post*, April 13, 1989, p. A33

the environment. But these laws focus more on managing the wastes after they're created than on minimizing their danger to the environment or eliminating them entirely.

One environmental group, Citizens for a Better Environment, proposes a long-term reduction of toxic wastes at their source. They support a two-pronged approach to the reduction of toxic waste: educating the consumer to make environmentally sound choices and pressuring manufacturers

Hazardous waste remains a threat to the environment long after it's sealed in 55-gallon drums.

to change their materials, processes, and end products to reduce the generation of toxic waste. In the meantime, scientists are working to develop biologically safe ways to rid the environment of existing toxic wastes.

For decades, Minnesota sawmills have been dumping the wood preservative pentachlorophenol (penta) into open pits scattered across the land. Today, the toxic chemical is turning up in the groundwater supplies of several towns and communities. The question is, how do they get rid of it?

In an effort to find an answer, University of Minnesota scientists are studying more than 500 penta pits across the nation to determine if bacteria can be used to clean up the hazardous wastes. Bacteria have been used in some areas to clean up municipal wastewater for nearly a century. But biochemists now believe that nature may also be able to provide organisms capable of digesting some of the world's most troublesome toxins.

The specific microbe being tested in Minnesota is called Flavo bacterium. Ron Crawford of the university's Gray Freshwater Biological Institute recently isolated the bacterium by feeding it a sample of penta-fouled soil.

"Over a period of several months," says Crawford, "any organism that can't metabolize penta will not survive." But Flavo bacterium is surviving quite nicely, turning penta into less harmful carbon dioxide and chlorides in the process.

Another researcher at the university, John Wood, is experimenting with algae that can convert toxic heavy metals such as lead and mercury into less harmful compounds. The process doesn't eliminate the metals from the environment, but it does prevent them from doing further damage by keeping them out of the food chain.

In still another promising development, Michigan State University biochemists Steven D. Aust and John A. Bumpus have discovered that the same enzymes that are responsible for the decomposition of dead trees are also capable of reducing several deadly and persistent poisons such as DDT, lindane, PCBs, and dioxin into carbon dioxide.

The results of these and other successful lab tests show the feasibility of using biological organisms to cleanse the environment. Still unclear, however, is whether or not these methods of control will find wide use anytime soon. As Sierra Club political director Carl Pope points out in the book, *Hazardous Wastes in America*, "The demand hasn't been there because it's cheaper just to dump the stuff."

TAKING STOCK

In our haste to feed a hungry world, in our greed to make a profit, in our ignorance and arrogance to turn what nature has created over millions of years into something better for ourselves, we're slowly but surely destroying the very land on which we live. In the process, we're affecting every living creature on Earth. The truth is that we simply can't continue doing what we're doing.

Throughout the upper Midwest, as well as in the rest of the country, it's necessary to stop to evaluate our actions before making any changes to the environment. We need to think before we act, even if we have only the best of intentions. Good intentions, after all, can destroy, too.

As the comic strip character Pogo once commented, "We have met the enemy, and he is us."

C H A P T E R T H R E E

THE AIR
WE BREATHE

The skies that make up a critical part of Earth's biosphere are filled with gases—mostly nitrogen and oxygen with trace amounts of carbon dioxide, helium, hydrogen, ozone, and argon.[1] These gases work together to provide the atmosphere necessary for life on Earth. At the same time they protect Earth's inhabitants from the harmful effects of solar radiation.

But something has happened to the chemical makeup of the atmosphere since the Industrial Revolution began. It's changed, and those changes are causing alarm among scientists around the world.

Carbon dioxide has risen from 0.028 percent to 0.035 percent in the last century.[2] Methane is likewise increasing at a rate that could cause it to double in the next century.

Although these increases may seem insignificant, they're large enough to cause serious concern. When combined with the by-products of an industrialized world—such pollutants as sulfur dioxide, particulates, carbon monoxide, nitrogen dioxide, chlorofluorocarbons, ozone, and lead, all flowing skyward at a phenomenal rate—the results are catastrophic. One of the most frightening consequences of these results is called the greenhouse effect.

(opposite page)
Airplanes monitor the atmosphere for signs of ozone and other pollutants.

THE GREENHOUSE EFFECT

Throughout the North Central states, such gases as chlorofluorocarbons (CFCs), methane, nitrogen oxides, and carbon dioxide (sometimes called the greenhouse gases) are produced by heavy industry, agriculture, and daily living. These gases concentrate in the atmosphere and prevent the sun's heat, radiated by the Earth, from escaping. As a result, Earth's temperatures climb steadily higher. In time, this rise in heat could create an overall increase in the planet's average temperatures of from 2 to 9°F.

Rising temperatures, in turn, could reduce global rainfall, trigger worldwide droughts, create coastal flooding, and spark global famine. Even minor reductions in annual rainfall in the already dry North Central areas of Nebraska, South Dakota, and southwestern Iowa could spell disaster for both plants and animals. Increases in atmospheric temperatures could kill thousands of species of plants and animals.[3]

Although the EPA has devised a six-point plan to reduce the amount of greenhouse gases in the atmosphere, scientists doubt that the plan will have much effect on the environment at least until the twenty-second century. By then, the overall buildup of greenhouse gases may already have raised Earth's temperature by 1 to 2°F.[4]

U.S. Sources of Carbon Dioxide Emissions

Electric Utilities	33%
Transportation	31%
Industry	24%
Buildings	12%

Source: MacKenzie, *Breathing Easier* p.10

ACID RAIN

Acid rain is another serious problem affecting the North Central states. When carbon dioxide is dissolved in moisture in the air, it forms a compound called carbonic acid. As sulfur dioxide, nitrogen oxides, and hydrogen sulfides from burning fossil fuels such as coal, oil, and gasoline combine with the carbonic acid, they create corrosive sulfuric or nitric acids. These acids can be extremely harmful to living organisms.

But the acids in acid rain cause more than an air pollution problem. Concentrated acids in the atmosphere eventually settle to Earth with rain and dust. The result is acidified lakes, rivers, and streams from one end of the Midwest to the other. Aquatic plants and animals, unable to survive in acidic water, are dying.

Acid rain also takes its toll on marble, limestone, bronze, and sandstone. Statues in Chicago's Lincoln Park are steadily eroding due to acid rain, and cemetery tombstones have become unreadable. Millions of dollars are being spent each year to repair acid rain damage to buildings in such major metropolitan areas as Detroit, Cleveland, Cincinnati, and Minneapolis.[5]

(opposite page)
Beautiful lakes like this one in central Wisconsin are slowly dying from acid rain pollution.

Even though acid rain often begins in the large cities of the upper Midwest, it soon becomes an international problem. Prevailing winds carry many of the acidic compounds from the Upper Great Lakes region through the Ohio River valley east. Pollutants entering the atmosphere from a coal-fired power plant in Cleveland or Chicago may eventually fall to Earth and kill off brown trout in upstate New York or southeastern Canada. The EPA estimates that more than 4,000 lakes in the United States and 164,000 in Canada are already so badly acidified that aquatic life is threatened or has already disappeared. And the number of acidified lakes grows larger each day.

ALL SMOGGED IN

Like acid rain, smog—the airborne pollutants that come from industrial smokestacks and automobile engine emissions—is a serious problem in and around major cities throughout the North Central region.

During the long, hot summer of 1988, America's air turned thick with smog that was produced by sunlight acting on such airborne pollutants as automobile exhaust fumes and ozone. While East and West Coast cities such as Los Angeles, New York, and San Diego are used to dealing with smog, a number of North Central cities that had rarely been plagued by the problem were suddenly faced with the worst smog in a decade.

Detroit battled ozone levels far above federal health standards on more days in 1988 than in any year since 1978 and nearly ten times as many as in 1987. Ozone pollution in Chicago reached serious levels on twice as many days in 1988 as in 1987, soaring frequently to nearly twice the federal standards and triggering the city's first major smog alerts in over a decade. Smog-fouled air not only creates a breathing problem for Earth's inhabitants but also does a minimum of $5 billion of damage to U.S. crops annually.[6]

In response to growing concern over urban smog levels, Congress in 1977 passed amendments to the Clean Air Act. These amendments required all U.S. cities to attain certain air-quality standards within ten years. But by 1987, more than a hundred cities still hadn't met those requirements, so Congress granted an extension to August 31, 1988.

Today, smog remains a serious health hazard in numerous cities throughout the upper Midwest. But there's some good news, too. The EPA reported in 1988 that the average level of lead in the nation's air had dropped 35 percent, due primarily to a nationwide switch to unleaded automobile fuels. That's the largest single decline since monitoring began in the early 1970s. Carbon monoxide emissions were also reduced.

Two small steps, perhaps, but a giant leap for the environment.

C H A P T E R F O U R

THE WATER WE DRINK

Water is necessary for life on Earth. Life began in the seas, and water has played a key role in the development of life ever since.

Yet, each day, the North Central United States is exposed to countless sources of water pollution. Lakes that have lived in harmony with the land for thousands of years are being threatened by chemical runoff and pollutants. Rivers and streams are being turned into cesspools as raw sewage and industrial wastes are piped into them. Even the Great Lakes—the largest continuous freshwater body in the world—are staggering beneath the pressures humankind has placed on them.

CHEMICAL POLLUTANTS

Among the greatest threats to the upper Midwest are chemical pollutants—poisonous chemicals that escape into the environment and may remain toxic for years or even decades. Nowhere is the problem more serious than in the Great Lakes.

All five Great Lakes—Erie, Huron, Superior, Ontario, and Michigan—are in trouble. Two hundred years of exploitation and another hundred years of abuse have turned the world's largest reservoir of fresh water into a sink for toxic chemicals. The impact on Great Lakes residents is enormous.

Over 40 million people live in the Great Lakes basin. More than 26 million of them draw their drinking water from the lakes. One fifth of America's industrial activities and half of Canada's take place there.

All this industrial development didn't happen overnight. In the mid-1800s, logging companies moved through the region,

(opposite page)
Lake Michigan–one of the five Great Lakes–is showing serious signs of toxic pollution.

37

destroying thousands of square miles of virgin forest in an operation known as the Big Cut. At about the same time, the fur industry entered the region, wiping out most of the area's fur-bearing wildlife.

A century later, with the completion of the canals connecting the Great Lakes with the northern Atlantic Ocean in the east, lamprey eels invaded the lakes and destroyed much of the commercial fishing industry. Between 1946 and 1966, two thirds of the region's fishing business disappeared.

Today, the area is plagued by a different problem. Poisonous, long-lasting chemicals pour into the water from the cities, farms, and industries rimming the lakes. Within walking distance of Cornwall Island in the middle of the St. Lawrence River, which carries Great Lakes water to the Atlantic, are such polluters as the Domtar pulp and paper mill, the CIL chemical company, Reynolds Aluminum, a General Motors foundry, British Cellophane, Ltd., the Cornwall sewage treatment plant, and Alcoa Aluminum, plus a number of toxic-waste dumps.

Eventually, every drop of water in the Great Lakes basin will pass by Cornwall Island on its way to the sea. Some of it will have passed through the municipal sewer system of Toronto, into which approximately 1,000 major industries pour their toxic wastes. Some of it will have picked up toxic polychlorinated biphenyls (PCBs) from the bed of Waukegan Harbor, one of the most contaminated ports in the nation. Some will have been piped through Dow Chemical's Midland, Michigan, plant, after being contaminated by highly toxic dioxins and more than 200 other dangerous chemical compounds. Some will have leached from the injection wells of Kimberly-Clark's paper mill on the shores of Lake Superior.

POLLUTION'S HEAVY TOLL

As a result of all this pollution, many of the turtles in the area contain excessively high concentrations of heavy metals, pesticides, and toxic chemicals in their flesh. PCBs in snapping turtle flesh top 800 parts per million (ppm). Officials consider PCB concentrations above 50 ppm hazardous. One shrew was found to contain PCBs equal to 1 percent of its body weight—or more than 11,000 ppm!

Liver tumors, undiscovered in fish prior to 1964, now appear in a significant percentage of fish in the basin's rivers. Approximately half the birds living in Lake Michigan's Saginaw Bay show some form of physical defect, and most of the lake gulls suffer from goiter, a thyroid disease, as a result of constant exposure to the pollutants.

Herring gull eggs contain levels of the pesticide Mirex and PCBs in concentrations up to 25 million times higher than in the surrounding waters. Many of these gulls are born with deformities such as misshapen bills, clubfeet, swollen skulls, and missing eyes. These and countless other tragedies are the result of the contamination of the Great Lakes.

So far, nearly 500 chemicals have been detected in Great Lakes fish. A 1981 Fish and Wildlife Service study revealed that nearly every fish sampled contained detectable amounts of DDT, PCBs, and the pesticides toxaphene, dieldrin, and chlordane. And the pollution, for the most part, is getting worse instead of better.

CLEANING UP THE GREAT LAKES

What's happening to the Great Lakes is a microcosm of what's happening in the rest of the nation. Of more than 70,000 chemicals currently in use throughout North America, fewer than 2 percent have been studied closely enough to make a complete assessment of their hazards to the environment. Fifty thousand more have never been tested at all.

"If we continue acting as we do now," says Joyce McLean, of the Great Lakes Campaign for Greenpeace in Toronto, Canada, "we can only stumble blindly from crisis to crisis, trying to reverse the mistakes of the past."

Throughout the years, numerous attempts by the government to clean up the Great Lakes have been made, but few have been successful. This is partly because of the great amount of political power wielded by the giant industries dumping toxic wastes into the lakes and partly because of the inefficiency in enforcing governmental regulations. Passing laws governing the discharge of pollutants into the lakes has been easy. Seeing that they're carried out has been nearly impossible.

The ultimate responsibility for the cleanup of the Great Lakes basin may well rest with the people who live there, along with such action-oriented environmental groups as Greenpeace, Great Lakes United, and the Canadian Environmental Law Institute.

"At this point," according to Dr. Lynton K. Caldwell, Professor of Public Environmental Affairs at Indiana University, "environmentally concerned people and their governments face a task as difficult as humans have ever faced—the changing of human behavior."

HOPE FOR THE FUTURE

Toxic-chemical levels in the Great Lakes have already led to a U.S. ban on the sale of several species of Great Lakes fish. By the late 1970s, Lake Erie had become one of the most seriously polluted lakes in the world.

Toxic chemicals and discharges from sewage-treatment plants had all but killed Lake Erie. The most desirable species of fish had disappeared, and the water was filled with high concentrations of microorganisms and algae.[1]

The pollution came from Erie with its paper industries; Buffalo with its flour and chemicals; Cleveland with its petrochemicals and steel; Toledo with its glass and steel; and Detroit with its automobiles, steel, and paper.[2]

Today, Lake Erie is making a remarkable comeback. Salmon and trout once again inhabit the lake. The annual catch of commercial fish from the lake continues to rise, and toxic-chemical levels in the lake's predatory fish continue to fall.

In 1986, the eight states and two Canadian provinces bordering the Great Lakes signed the Toxic Substances Control Agreement. This agreement is designed to reduce toxic discharges into the lakes "to the maximum extent possible."

Under the agreement, discharges from the Niagara River into Lake Superior, for example, are to be cut in half by 1995. An agreement between Michigan and the Canadian province of Ontario requires both to work toward eliminating toxic compounds from the areas bordering their lakes. The result? Hundreds of millions of dollars and more than a decade later, the Great Lakes are slowly showing renewed signs of life.

INLAND LAKES SUFFER

In Wisconsin's lower Fox River, a 40-mile inland waterway between Lake Winnebago and Green Bay, chemical pollutants from 20 pulp and paper mills located along the lake had destroyed nearly all the river's aquatic life. Paper waste coated the banks, and dyes and sewage discolored the water.

In 1972, Congress passed the Clean Water Act, which limited waste discharges and set water-quality standards in the Fox and other waterways. But the sheer volume of treated sewage and chemical discharges exceeded the river's ability to recover.

Once one of the most polluted waterways in Wisconsin, today the Fox River is showing signs of healing.

In a last-ditch effort to save the Fox, the Wisconsin Department of Natural Resources began monitoring the river's vital signs, including temperature and oxygen levels. The department limited each factory and sewage plant along the river to a maximum level of discharge each day.

Today, the once-infamous Fox is slowly showing signs of healing. One of the surest signs? Fishermen are once again taking trophy-size walleyes from the river, and recreational boats ply its newly restored waters.[3]

FOSSIL-FUEL POLLUTANTS

The energy industry, too, contributes heavily to water pollution. Oil spilled from ships or deliberately dumped during routine cleaning procedures has resulted in the deaths of thousands of seabirds and other forms of Great Lakes life.

As oil from a spill washes ashore, it forms a thick, tar-like skin, choking off all life. The oil destroys the feeding and breeding habitats of countless species of fish, birds, small animals, and insects and can cost millions of dollars to clean up.

Yet, as more oil is shipped across the Great Lakes, the number of vessels hauling it increases—increasing, too, the chances for a disastrous offshore oil spill. Offshore drilling in all five Great Lakes has been banned under the Toxic Substances Control Agreement. However, the possibility of oil pollution remains great.

GOING UNDERGROUND

Throughout the upper Midwest, supplies of groundwater—water stored within the pores of soil and rock formations—are slowly being poisoned by chemical and other hazardous wastes. One out of every two wells in rural Dane County, outside the state capital of Madison, Wisconsin, is currently contaminated with the agricultural chemical atrizine, a pesticide used principally in the production of corn. Like many other groundwater pollutants, atrizine is carcinogenic, or cancer-causing.

The result is that the North Central states are losing their clean water supplies at a staggering rate while countless species of fish, waterfowl, amphibians, reptiles, and aquatic plants are dying off. And the saddest part is that the entire country could eliminate much of its pesticide-contamination problem practically overnight.

INTEGRATED PEST MANAGEMENT

The U.S. Department of Agriculture has monitored various integrated pest management (IPM) methods that rely on biology to control pests. One such method is the use of natural predators to eliminate pests. Another is a change in crop planting practices. A third is the genetic modification of plants to resist pests more effectively.

For some 40 crops, the department found IPM to be economically beneficial. Farmers using IPM methods in 15 states realized profits nearly $600 million greater than they would have shown without using IPM, all the while reducing the amount of toxic pesticides applied to fields.[4]

Recent studies show that decreasing the use of pesticides in the United States by as much as one half by relying on currently available pest-management strategies makes economic sense. The program would cost farmers and consumers an estimated $830 million a year and would increase the cost of food to consumers by less than 0.2 percent.

Nonchemical methods can be used to control the spread of weeds, too. Such agricultural practices as intercropping—or growing two or more crop varieties together—can suppress weed growth while adding nitrogen to the soil. Using certain cover crops that deter weed growth by releasing natural toxins is also effective. Likewise, mulches, including the residues of some crops, can reduce weed growth while minimizing the use of chemical herbicides.[5]

All these methods offer the added benefit of preventing chemical fertilizers, insecticides, and herbicides from entering groundwater systems. As people gradually come to understand the importance of maintaining clean water sources, progress is being made, if ever so slowly.

A TIME FOR ACTION

Throughout the North Central states, humanity has shown a deadly mixture of ignorance, laziness, and greed that has driven countless species of plants and animals to extinction. The list of endangered species in the upper Midwest alone includes birds such as the prairie chicken and bald eagle; large land mammals such as the southern and northern bison, pronghorn antelope, bighorn sheep, elk, timber wolf, and grizzly bear; small mammals such as the northern kit fox, black-footed ferret, and several varieties of bats; and fish such as the freshwater sturgeon, blue pike, and longjaw cisco. Nearly 8 percent of all plant species are likewise endangered, according to the Center for Plant Conservation. As many as 700 species nationwide may become extinct by the year 2000.

Luckily, not everyone living in the North Central states takes the region's wildlife for granted. Each and every day, someone new joins the battle to help save the environment.

PUTTING COMPOST TO WORK

Nearly 20 percent of the waste generated in the upper Midwest is composed of organic, or once-living, material such as grass clippings, leaves, twigs, straw, garden refuse, and household vegetable wastes. When organic material is put in the trash, nature loses the nutrients that were originally intended to be returned to the Earth.

North Central farmers have used compost as a means of improving their soils' fertility ever since settling the prairie lands more than a century ago. Advances in chemical fertilizers, however, eventually turned many farmers away from

(opposite page)
The number of endangered species in the North Central region–like this bald eagle–continues to climb annually.

organic materials. Spraying a 300-acre field with liquid nitrogen from giant tanks is easier and cheaper than returning used cornstalks, straw, and other agricultural waste products to the fields. At least that's what agricultural chemical manufacturers have been saying for years.

But in 1980, Minnesota passed one of the most progressive waste-management acts of any state. The act was designed to eliminate large amounts of trash in landfills while finding alternative uses for these "disposables."

In Wisconsin's Portage County, just across the Mississippi River from Minnesota, a revolutionary project involving agricultural compost has become a worldwide showcase. The project demonstrates that, by using compost that was once burned or landfilled as trash, farmers can increase crop yields, lower expenses, and improve the quality of the environment—all with little or no more effort than by conventional methods relying on chemical fertilizers.

"We just decided we'd had enough," said one Portage County farmer involved with the project. "While the chemical companies slowly strangled us with increasing prices, our fields were growing less and less productive. That meant more and more chemical fertilizers. It was a never-ending chain."

Today, an increasing number of farmers throughout the North Central states are turning to a minimum-till or no-till method of farming that returns crop waste to the land or leaves it there following harvest. Continuing agricultural department studies show increases in soil fertility and decreases in chemical runoff, salinization (excess salts in the soil), and other forms of pollution.

"The beauty of composting," according to author Jon Naar in his book *Design for a Livable Planet*, "is that it can be done from virtually any biodegradable waste in almost any quantity. Its full potential, as the basis of organic food growing and as an inexpensive yet highly marketable replacement for synthetic fertilizers, is only now becoming widely appreciated."[1]

NEW-AGE ENVIRONMENTALIST

At first glance, Wes Birdsall might seem like just another environmentalist. When the 1974 Arab oil embargo threatened U.S.

oil supplies and sent energy prices soaring, Birdsall hit the streets in Osage, Iowa, preaching a message of conservation. What's unusual is that Birdsall is general manager of Osage Municipal Utilities, Inc., a supplier of electricity and natural gas to a town of 3,800 people.

Although environmentalists within the energy industry are rare, Birdsall began speaking to groups about conserving energy. His company established a residential insulation program for low-income homeowners. The utility set strict building standards that new customers had to meet to get service. Birdsall also led a drive to install more efficient lights on Main Street.

Osage Municipal practiced what it preached. The company checked its own facilities and power lines to detect losses and made various improvements to conserve power. It also handed out water-heater insulation jackets to Osage residents, 95 percent of which now have insulated heaters.

The company gave away money-saving compact fluorescent light bulbs. Each bulb saves an estimated 400 pounds of coal over the average life span of a typical incandescent bulb.

The results of Birdsall's efforts have been impressive. Increased efficiency saved Osage an estimated $1.2 million in 1988. Demands for electricity have risen less than 3 percent a year since 1974, even though Osage's population and commercial activity have grown at a higher rate. Use of natural gas for heating has fallen 37 percent. Decreased energy consumption means less power that Osage must purchase from out-of-state—a savings that the utilities company has passed along to its customers through lower bills. Rates were cut 5 times for a total of 19 percent from 1982 to 1988.

Says Birdsall, "Our first thought was to keep the money in our community. Helping the environment was an offshoot of it. Yeah, I guess I am [an environmentalist]. We should all be looking out for the environment."[2]

CHEATING EXTINCTION

"If you've seen 15 whooping cranes," says David Day in his book *The Environmental Wars*, "you've seen them all." Back in the early 1940s, that statement was literally true.

Forced to the very brink of extinction by hunters seeking their magnificent plumes, whooping cranes were granted government protection in 1942. But by 1962, after two full decades, their number had risen to only 28. Although that was an improvement, all 28 birds belonged to a single flock that migrated annually some 2,600 miles from Canada to southern Texas. One savage storm, one major toxic disaster, or a group of misguided hunters could have wiped the colony out.

Then, in 1977, crane researchers George Archibald and Ron Sauer founded the International Crane Foundation (ICF) in Baraboo, Wisconsin. Using artificial insemination, the two set about reversing the cranes' decline.

Befriending the cranes and dancing the ritual whooping-crane mating dances that the researchers had observed during years of study, Archibald was eventually able to coax a single female into laying an egg. Two-and-a-half weeks later, the egg hatched. The baby whooper—the first ever hatched under such strange circumstances—was named Gee Whiz.

By closely observing whooping crane behavior and relying on innovative breeding and hatching techniques, ICF has since enjoyed numerous successes. By 1980, the foundation was rearing 25 endangered cranes a year. This included the rare Japanese red-crowned and the even rarer Siberian cranes.

Despite ICF's success in breeding captive cranes, Archibald realizes that such measures are merely first aid to revive a dying species. What the cranes need most is suitable natural habitat to ensure the survival of the species. Toward that end, the work of Archibald, Sauer, and the ICF has only begun.[3]

THE BIRTH OF "ECOTAGE"

In 1970, Environmental Action, a Washington, D.C.–based anti-pollution group, coordinated the first Earth Day celebration. The group coined the term *ecotage* to describe any act of sabotage aiding the cause of ecology.

The world's first environmental rebel was known during the mid-1960s as "The Fox." Mike Royko, then a columnist for the *Chicago Daily Express* and The Fox's media contact, described the masked rebel as an "anti-pollution Zorro who has been harassing various companies, evading the police, and making himself a minor legend around Aurora and Kane County [Illinois]."

Motivated by outrage at various industries that were polluting the Fox River and neighboring countryside, The Fox wore many disguises to conceal his true identity. Once he collected a sample of river sludge and dead fish near a chemical company's discharge pipe, walked into the corporate offices of the company, and dumped the gooey contents in the center of the company's shimmering white carpet.

In other escapades, The Fox blocked factory sewage and drainage systems and sealed off polluting smokestacks. Wherever he struck, he left a note warning the company to "clean up your act" and signed it, "The Fox."

These and other acts of ecotage were often followed by a poster campaign against offending corporations. During one such campaign, posters and stickers attacking U.S. Steel, one of the area's major polluters, appeared everywhere. One sign more than 60 feet long appeared one morning on a railway bridge above the Indiana toll road. Mimicking U.S. Steel's motto, "We're involved," the sign read, "U.S. Steel: We're Involved—in Killing Lake Michigan."

Although The Fox has since retired from active duty, his memory serves as a role model for other eco-command groups. [4]

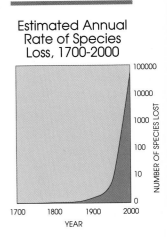

Estimated Annual Rate of Species Loss, 1700-2000

Source: Based on estimates in Norman Myers (Ed., Gaia: An Atlas of Planet Management (Garden City, NY: Anchor Books, 1984), p. 155

WHAT WE CAN DO

There are numerous things we can do to help preserve the North Central states' environment. Although not all the following steps are absolutely non-polluting, they're some of the best ideas the nation's environmentalists have devised so far to stop the spread of pollution.

FOR THE LAND

- Learn about local recycling programs. If none exists, create one. Contact nearby recycling groups, private recyclers, and national recycling organizations.

- Locate and use nearby markets and collection points for paper, glass, metals, and plastics. For information about recycling plastics, call 1-800-542-7780 toll free.

- Organize roadside walks to collect cans, bottles, and other recyclable trash.

- Organize community pickups of recyclable materials.

- If you have a yard or garden, compost yard and vegetable wastes.

- Obtain recycled printing and writing paper for your home or school through a local printer or paper distributor. Recycled paper is most commonly available in the Midwest, where most of it is made. For more information, contact the Earth Care Paper Company at 608-256-5522 or Prairie Paper at 402-477-0825.

- Form a consumer group with your neighbors or classmates and buy pesticide-free organic foods in bulk from your local

(opposite page)
Once each decade, people assemble to celebrate Earth Day and to discuss what everyone can do to help the environment.

natural-foods store. Ask local grocery stores and supermarket chains to begin carrying organic products.

- Avoid environmentally harmful home products. Ask retailers about alternatives. You may be able to control a pest problem without using a pesticide, for example.

- Pour hazardous liquids such as cleaning fluids into a plastic container that's filled with kitty litter or stuffed with newspaper. Close the top securely, and dispose of the container properly at a hazardous-waste disposal site.

- Take used motor oil and antifreeze to a gas station with an oil-recycling program.

- Add to your yard natural predators such as ladybugs, lacewings, mantises, toads, and garter snakes to eat insect pests.

- Buy plants that are pest- and disease-resistant.

- Plant more trees—including deciduous shade trees—to protect west-facing windows from the summer sun.

FOR THE WATER

- Save an average of 2,900 to 5,800 gallons of water a year by having your parents install a displacement bag or toilet dam in your toilet tank. Or make one yourself by hanging a gallon-size filled, sealed plastic bag inside the tank.

- If you must water your lawn, do so in early morning to prevent evaporation from the hot sun.

- Use only "clean" detergents—those low in polluting phosphates. Most liquid detergents are phosphate-free, as are soap flakes.

- Use drought-resistant plant varieties in your garden. Cactus and succulents require little water, as do hundreds of species of colorful flowers such as wisteria, sweet alyssum, and daffodil.

- Have your parents install sink-faucet aerators and water-saving shower heads to reduce water usage up to 80 percent without decreasing performance.

- Ask your parents to insulate your hot-water heater and turn its thermostat down to 120°.

IN GENERAL

- Start a public education program on local environmental issues and invite local experts to speak at meetings—either at your home or in your school hall.

- Reduce the amount of materials you use and buy. Purchase items with the least amount of packaging. Wash out and reuse containers—even plastic bags—whenever possible.

- Establish paper-collection points in school and arrange for periodic pickups, or have the paper delivered to a local recycling center.

- Buy in bulk whenever possible to save on packaging.

- Work with your community to organize a household hazardous-waste collection program.

- Join a national or an international organization working to protect the environment and control hazardous waste.

- Handle household chemicals with extreme care. Make sure you read the label to know what the potential hazards are.

- Buy beverages in returnable glass containers.

- Encourage your parents to get a low-cost home-energy audit from your local utility company. Follow all suggestions on improving the energy efficiency of your house.

- Turn down the thermostat at night and whenever the house is empty and close off heat or air conditioning ducts in unoccupied rooms.

- Dry clothes on a clothesline instead of in a dryer.

- Eat lower on the food chain—more fruit, vegetables, and grains and less meat, fish, and animal products.

- Avoid aerosols and other products containing chlorofluorocarbons (CFCs) that are damaging to the environment.

- Join at least one environmental organization whose goals and activities you support.

FOR MORE INFORMATION

The following toll-free hot-line telephone numbers provide information ranging from pesticide use to asbestos in homes; from hazardous-waste disposal to chemical-emergency preparedness.

- Asbestos Hotline (1-800-334-8571). Provides information on asbestos and asbestos abatement programs; Mon. to Fri., 8:15 a.m. to 5 p.m.

- Chemical Emergency Preparedness Program Hotline (1-800-535-0202). For information on community preparedness for chemical accidents, etc.; Mon. to Fri., 8:30 a.m. to 4:30 p.m.

- Inspector General's Whistle Blower Hotline (1-800-424-4000). For confidential reporting of EPA-related waste, fraud, abuse, or mismanagement; Mon. to Fri., 10 a.m. to 3 p.m.

- National Pesticides Telecommunications Network Hotline (1-800-858-7378). Provides information about pesticides, toxicity, management, health and environmental effects, safety practices, and cleanup and disposal; 7 days, 24 hours a day.

- National Response Center Hotline (1-800-424-8802). For reporting oil and hazardous chemical spills; 7 days, 24 hours a day.

- Superfund Hotline (1-800-424-9346). Provides Superfund information and technical assistance; Mon. to Fri., 8:30 a.m. to 4:30 p.m.

The following list includes organizations that can provide information and materials on various topics of environmental concern to the North Central region.

(opposite page)
Windmills are only one source of alternative energy that could reduce the region's reliance on polluting fossil fuels.

American Water
  Resources Association
5410 Grosvenor Lane
Bethesda, MD 20814
301-492-8600

Center for Clean Air
  Policy
444 N. Capitol St.
Washington, D.C. 20001
202-624-7709

Citizen's Clearinghouse
  for Hazardous Wastes
P.O. Box 926
Arlington, VA 22216
703-276-7070

Citizens for a Better
  Environment
59 E. Van Buren St., Suite
  1600
Chicago, IL 60605
312-939-1530

Common Cause
2030 M St. NW
Washington, D.C. 20036
202-833-1200

The Conservation
  Foundation
1250 23rd St. NW
Washington, D.C. 20037
202-293-4800

Consumer Products
  Safety Commission
  (CPSC)
Central Regional Center
230 S. Dearborn St., Rm.
  2944
Chicago, IL 60604
312-353-8260

Council for Solid Waste
  Solutions
1275 K St. NW
Washington, D.C. 20005
202-371-5319

Council on
  Environmental Quality
722 Jackson Place NW
Washington, D.C. 20006
202-395-5750

Defenders of Wildlife
1244 19th St. NW
Washington, D.C. 20036
202-659-9510

Environmental Action
1525 New Hampshire
  Ave. NW
Washington, D.C. 20036
202-745-4870

Environmental Coalition
  for North America
1325 G St. NW
Washington, D.C. 20005
202-289-5009

Environmental Defense
  Fund
257 Park Ave. S.
New York, NY 10010
212-505-2100

Environmental
  Protection Agency
  (EPA)
Region V (IL, IN, MI,
  MN, OH, WI)
230 S. Dearborn St.
Chicago, IL 60604
312-353-2000

Friends of the Earth
530 7th St. SE
Washington, D.C. 20003
202-543-4312

Greenpeace USA
1436 U St. NW
Washington, D.C. 20009
202-462-1177

Izaak Walton League
1401 Wilson Blvd.
Arlington, VA 22209
703-528-1818

Keep America
  Beautiful, Inc.
Mill River Plaza
9 W. Broad St.
Stamford, CT 06902
(Phone # unavailable)

National Association for
  Plastic Container
  Recovery
5024 Parkway Plaza
  Blvd.
Charlotte, NC 28217
704-357-3250

National Audubon
  Society
950 Third Ave.
New York, NY 10022
212-832-3200

National Clean Air
  Coalition
530 Seventh St. SE
Washington, D.C. 20003
202-543-8200

National Coalition
  against the Misuse of
  Pesticides
530 7th St. SE
Washington, D.C. 20003
202-543-5450

National Geographic
  Society
17th and M Streets NW
Washington, D.C. 20036
202-857-7000

National Recycling
  Coalition
45 Rockefeller Plaza
New York, NY 10111
212-765-1800

National Wildlife
  Federation
1412 16th St. NW
Washington, D.C. 20036
202-737-2024

The Nature Conservancy
1815 N. Lynn St.
Arlington, VA 22209
703-841-5300

People Against
  Hazardous Landfill
  Sites (PAHLS)
P.O. Box 37
608 Highway 130
Wheeler, IN 46393
219-465-7466

Sierra Club
530 Bush St.
San Francisco, CA 94108
415-981-8634

Soil and Water
 Conservation Society
7515 Northeast Ankeny
 Rd.
Ankeny, IA 50021-9764
(Phone # unavailable)

United Nations
 Environment Program
2 U. N. Plaza
New York, NY 10022
212-963-8139

U.S. Dept. of Agriculture
Independence Ave.
 between 12th and 14th
 Streets SW
Washington, D.C. 20250
202-477-8732

U.S. Environmental
 Protection Agency
401 M St. SW
Washington, D.C. 20460
202-382-2090

U.S. Fish and Wildlife
 Service
Dept. of the Interior
Washington, D.C. 20240
202-343-1100

U.S. Forest Service
P.O. Box 96090
Washington, D.C. 20090
202-447-3957

Wilderness Society
1400 Eye St. NW
Washington, D.C. 20005
202-833-2300

World Wildlife Fund
1250 24th St. NW
Washington, D.C. 20037
202-293-4800

N O T E S

INTRODUCTION

1. *The Universal Almanac 1990* (Kansas City, MO: Universal Press Syndicate Company, 1989), pp. 342 - 343.

CHAPTER ONE: THE WEB OF LIFE

1. David Rains Wallace, *Life in the Balance* (New York: Harcourt Brace Jovanovich, Publishers, 1987), p. 74.
2. *As We Live and Breathe,* National Geographic Society, 1971, p. 13.

CHAPTER TWO: THE LAND WE WALK

1. *The Global Ecology Handbook* (Boston: Beacon Press, 1990), p. 266.

CHAPTER THREE: THE AIR WE BREATHE

1. *The Universal Almanac 1990*, p. 332.
2. Ibid, p. 370.
3. Ibid, pp. 370-371.
4. Ibid, p. 371.
5. *The Global Ecology Handbook*, pp. 225-227.
6. Ruth Caplan, *Our Earth, Ourselves* (New York: Bantam Books, 1990), pp. 85-86.

CHAPTER FOUR: THE WATER WE DRINK

1. Richard H. Wagner, *Environment and Man* (New York: W. W. Norton & Company, 1974), p. 117.
2. Ibid, p. 117.
3. Wesley Marx, "Environmental Countdown," *Reader's Digest*, May 1990, p. 102.
4. *The Global Ecology Handbook*, p. 84.
5. Ibid, p. 84.

CHAPTER SIX: WHAT WE CAN DO

1. Jon Naar, *Design for a Livable Planet* (New York: Harper & Row, 1990), p. 24.
2. Caplan, *Our Earth, Ourselves*, pp. 48 - 49.
3. David Day, *The Environmental Wars* (New York: St. Martin's Press, 1989), pp. 154 - 156.
4. Ibid, pp. 216 - 217.

G L O S S A R Y

Acid rain. Rain containing a high concentration of acids from various pollutants such as sulfur dioxide, nitrogen oxide, etc.

Air pollution. The transfer of contaminating substances into the atmosphere, usually as a result of human activities.

Algae. Primitive green plants, many of which are microscopic.

Aquatic. Of or relating to life in the water.

Aquifer. Water-bearing rock or soil.

Atmosphere. A mass of gases surrounding the Earth.

Biological control. The use of a pest's natural predators and parasites to control its population.

Biome. A specific type of environment capable of supporting life.

Biosphere. That part of the Earth, including its atmosphere, in which life can exist.

Carcinogen. A substance known to cause cancer.

Compost. A fertilizer made up of organic materials.

Compound. A substance with fixed composition and containing more than one element.

Drought. A prolonged period of time without rain.

Dust. Tiny particulate materials that are primarily the product of wind erosion of soil.

Ecosystem. A functioning unit of the environment that includes all living organisms and physical features within a given area.

Ecotage. Various acts of protest against environmental polluters.

Energy. The ability to perform work.

Erosion. The removal and transportation of soil by wind, running water, or glaciation.

Extinction. The disappearance of an organism from Earth.

Fertilizer. A substance used to make soil more productive.

Food chain accumulation. An increase in the concentration of various chemicals in a food chain.

Fossil fuels. Various fuel materials such as coal, oil, and natural gas created from the remains of once-living organisms.

Fungus. Primitive plants such as mushrooms, blights, and rusts.

Glacier. A large body of ice moving slowly down a slope or spreading outward on a land surface.

Greenhouse effect. The increase in solar-radiated infrared light waves in Earth's atmosphere; the increase is caused by an accumulation of such gases as carbon dioxide and methane.

Groundwater. Water that is contained in subsurface rock and soil formations.

Hazardous waste. The extremely dangerous by-product of civilization that, by its chemical makeup, is harmful to life.

Heavy metal. A metal such as mercury or lead that is harmful to life.

Herbicide. A chemical compound used to kill plants.

Irrigation. The process of diverting water from its source to farmland in order to increase crop yields.

Kettle hole. A steep-sided hollow without surface drainage, especially in a glaciated area.

Landfill. A site for the disposal of garbage and other waste products.

Leaching. The dissolving and transporting of materials by water seeping downward through soil.

Monoculture. The agricultural practice of growing only one variety of crop.

Nuclear waste. The long-lived, extremely dangerous by-product of nuclear energy or nuclear weapons production.

Particulates. Extremely small bits of dust, soot, soil, etc., that may become airborne.

PCBs. A group of highly toxic organic compounds once widely used as liquid coolants and insulators in industrial equipment.

Pesticide. A general term for any of a large number of chemical compounds used to kill pests such as insects, weeds, fungi, bacteria, etc.

Pollution. A general term for environmental contamination.

Recycling. The recovery and reuse of material resources.

Rock. Solid matter composed of one or more minerals.

Runoff. Water that runs across land as in a ditch, stream, or river.

Salinization. The increase of salt in soil or water.

Sewage. Refuse liquid or waste matter carried by sewers.

Smog. A visible mixture of solid, liquid, and gaseous air pollutants that are harmful both to human beings and to the environment.

Soil. A living system of weathered rock, organic matter, air, and water in which plants grow.

Strip-mining. A method of surface mining that takes in a wide area and is usually used for the removal of coal near the Earth's surface.

Swamp. Wet, spongy land saturated with and occasionally submerged beneath water.

Toxic waste. The extremely dangerous by-product of chemical production or use.

Urban sprawl. The spread of civilization out of urban and into rural areas.

Water pollution. The transfer of contaminating substances into water, usually as a result of human activities.

Water table. The highest level of a groundwater reservoir.

Wetlands. Land containing a high moisture content.

BIBLIOGRAPHY

"As Pollution Problems Spread, Communities Are Taking Action." *National Wildlife*, February/March 1989, p. 40.

As We Live and Breathe. Washington, D.C.: National Geographic Society, 1971.

Budiansky, Stephen, and Robert F. Black. "Tons and Tons of Trash and No Place To Put It." *U.S. News and World Report*, Dec. 14, 1987, pp. 58 - 62.

"Cropland Erosion Nears Crisis Levels in Many Areas of the Nation." *National Wildlife*, February/March 1989, p. 39.

"Drought and Wetlands Drainage Take a Heavy Toll on Many Species." *National Wildlife*, February/March 1989, p. 34.

The Earth Report. Los Angeles: Price Stern Sloan, Inc., 1988.

Grossman, Karl. *The Poison Conspiracy*. Sag Harbor, NY: The Permanent Press, 1983.

Marx, Wesley. "Environmental Countdown." *Reader's Digest*, May 1990, p. 99.

McLeod, Reggie. "Holmen Recycler Makes Reverse Process Work." *Wisconsin State Journal*, May 6, 1990, p. 5E.

Moran, Joseph M., Michael D. Morgan, and James H. Wiersma. *An Introduction to Environmental Sciences*. Boston: Little, Brown and Company, 1973.

"Record Ozone Levels and an Acid Rain Stalemate Obscure Progress." *National Wildlife*, February/March 1989, p. 35.

Toner, Mike. "Pollution Fighters Take to the Trees." *National Wildlife*, December/January 1987, p. 38.

Wagner, Richard H. *Environment and Man*. New York: W. W. Norton & Co., Inc., 1974.

Wallace, David Rains. *Life in the Balance*. New York: Harcourt Brace Jovanovich, 1987.

I N D E X

Acid rain 32, 33
Agricultural chemicals 22, 42, 46
Alcoa Aluminum Co. 38
Algae 22, 29, 40
Aquatic plants 8, 32, 43
Archibald, George 48
Argon 31
Audubon, John James 23
Aust, Steven D. 29

Bacteria 28
Badgers 11, 12, 18
Bald eagles 45
Biomes 7, 11
Biosphere 8, 9, 31
Birdsall, Wes 47
Bison 12, 45
Black-footed ferret 45
Blue pike 45
British Cellophane, Ltd. 38
Bumpus, John A. 29

Cache Basin Swamp 23
Caldwell, Lynton K. 40
Canadian Environmental Law Institute 40
Carbon dioxide 29, 31, 32
Carbon monoxide 31, 34
Carbonic acid 32
Center for Plant Conservation 45
Chemical pollutants 37, 41
Chicago 32, 33, 49
Chlordane 39
Chlorofluorocarbons [CFCs] 31
CIL Chemical Company 38
Cincinnati 32
Citizens for a Better Environment 27
Clean Air Act 33
Cleveland 32, 33, 40
Coal 22-23, 32, 33, 47
Compost 45
Cornwall sewage treatment plant 38
Cougars 23
Coyotes 7, 17, 18
Crawford, Ron 28-29
Cypress darter 24

Dane County 42
Day, David 47
DDT 29, 39
Design for a Livable Planet 46
Detroit 32, 33, 40
Dieldrin 39
Dinosaurs 8
Dioxin 29, 38
Domtar pulp and paper mill 38
Dow Chemical 38
Dust Bowl 15, 18, 21

East Missouri Sierra Club 25
Eastern ribbon snake 24
Environmental Action 49
Environmental Protection Agency 25, 26, 32, 33, 34
Environmental Wars, The 47
Erosion 14, 15, 21, 22

Fox River 41-42

Garbage 25
Gasoline 32
General Motors 38
Glaciers 8, 12
Gophers 11, 12
Government Accounting Office (GAO) 23
Grafton 18
Gray fox 17
Gray Freshwater Biological Institute 28
Great barred owls 17
Great Lakes 7, 8, 33, 37, 38, 39-40, 42
Great Lakes United 40
Green Bay 41
Greenhouse effect 31
Greenhouse gases 31-32
Greenpeace 39-40
Grizzly bear 45
Ground squirrels 12
Groundhogs 11

Hazardous Wastes in America 29
Heavy metals 9, 29, 38
Helium 31

Homestead Act of 1862 12, 14
Homo sapiens 9
Household waste 25
Hydrogen 31
Hydrogen sulfide 32

Ice age 8
Illinois 7, 8, 11, 14, 21, 22, 23, 24, 26, 49
Incinerators 26
Indiana 7, 8, 22, 26, 40, 49
Industrial Revolution 31
Insecticides 18, 43
Integrated pest management [IPM] 43
International Crane Foundation
  [ICF] 48-49
Iowa 7, 8, 12, 22, 32, 47
Ivory-billed woodpecker 23

Kimberly-Clark 38

Lake Erie 40
Lake Huron 37
Lake Michigan 39, 49
Lake Ontario 37
Lake Superior 37, 38, 40
Lake Winnebago 41
Lamprey eel 38
Landfills 26, 46
Lead 29, 31, 34
Lincoln Park 32
Lindane 29
Longjaw cisco 45

McLean, Joyce 39
Mercury 29
Methane 31
Michigan 7, 26, 29, 38, 40
Michigan State University 29
Minneapolis 32
Minnesota 7, 8, 26, 28, 46
Mirex 39
Mississippi River 7, 46
Monoculture 17, 18

Naar, Jon 46
Niagara River 40
Nitrogen dioxide 31
North Dakota 7, 18, 21
Northern kit fox 45

Offshore oil drilling 42
Ohio 7, 8, 11, 14, 22, 23, 26, 33
Ohio River Valley 33
Oil 12, 14, 15, 18, 21, 22, 23, 28, 32, 42,
  43, 45-47
Oil spills 42
Osage Municipal Utilities, Inc. 47
Ozone 31, 33

Particulates 31
Pentachlorophenol 28
Pesticides 18, 22, 38, 39, 42, 43
Phillippi, Ann 23
Polychlorinated Biphenyls [PCBs] 29, 38, 39
Polyculture 17
Pope, Carl 29
Prairie chicken 45
Pronghorn antelope 45

Recycling 25-26
Reynolds Aluminum 38
Riverport 24-25

Salinization 46
Salmon 40
Sierra Club 25, 29
Smog 33-34
St. Lawrence River 38
Strip-mining 22-23
Sturgeon 45
Sulfur dioxide 31, 32
Sulfuric acid 32

Tallgrass prairies 11-12
The Fox 41-42
Timber wolves 18
Toxaphene 39
Toxic Substances Control Agreement 40
Toxic waste 26-28, 38-39

U.S. Department of Agriculture 21, 43
U.S. Fish and Wildlife Service 25, 39
U.S. Steel 49
University of Minnesota 28

Waukegan Harbor 38
Whooping cranes 47-48
Wisconsin 7, 8, 12, 14, 25, 26, 41, 42, 46, 48
Wisconsin Department of Natural
  Resources 42